What Does a Dentist Do?

Heather Miller

Words to Know

cavity (KAH-vih-tee)—A bad spot in a tooth.

dental floss (DEN-tuhl FLAWSS)—A specially treated thread used to clean between teeth.

germs (JURMZ)—Very small living things that can cause someone to become sick.

gums (guhmz)—The skin around the teeth.

patient (PAY-shint)—The person being treated.

Enslow Elementary

an imprint of

Enslow Publishers, Inc.

40 Industrial Road   PO Box 38
Box 398   Aldershot
Berkeley Heights, NJ 07922   Hants GU12 6BP
USA   UK

http://www.enslow.com

Contents

The waiting room is empty at the beginning of the day.

Waiting to See the Dentist

The waiting room at the dentist's office will soon be filled with people. People of all ages will wait to see the dentist.

The dentist takes care of everyone's teeth. Some people will have a checkup and have their teeth cleaned.

safety glasses

gloves

mask

To keep us healthy, dentists and their helpers wear special things.

The Dentist Gets Ready

The dentist and his helper get ready. They take special care to get rid of germs. Germs can make people sick. They wash their hands with soap to kill germs. They put on gloves, safety glasses, and a mask to keep germs from spreading.

The patient is ready to see the dentist.

My Turn!

After sitting in the waiting room, it is now Jordan's turn.

The dentist's helper says,

"Jordan, we're ready to clean your teeth."

The dentist's helper uses a small mirror to check Jordan's teeth. The helper uses a special toothbrush to clean her teeth.

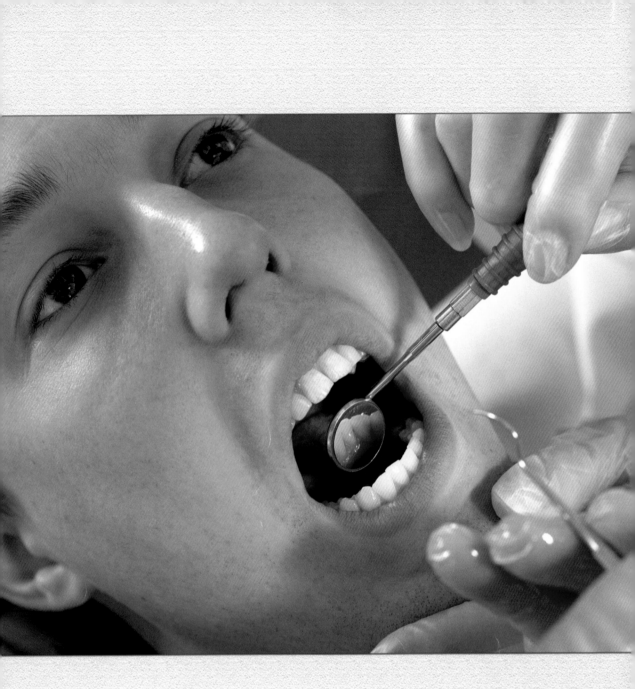

The dentist checks the backs of our teeth.

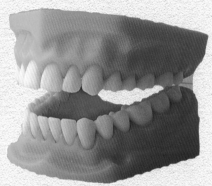

The dentist's helper gives Jordan a squirt of water. Jordan rinses her mouth. A special tube sucks the water away. Jordan's teeth are bright and clean. Jordan is ready to see the dentist.

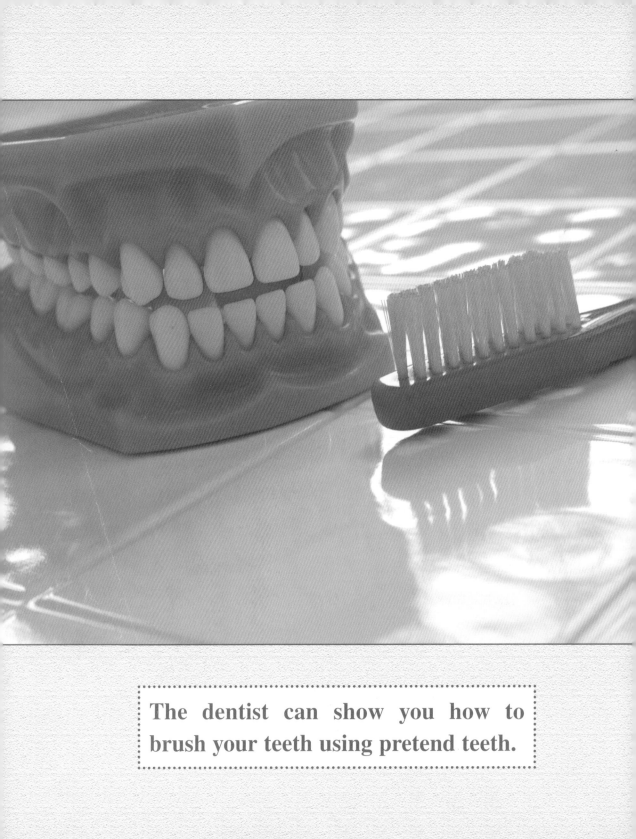

The dentist can show you how to brush your teeth using pretend teeth.

Where Do Dentists Learn?

Dentists have to go to a special school. First, they go to college for four years. They take a special test. Then they go to dental school. They learn all about teeth and gums. They practice on people's teeth. Now they are dentists.

The dentist checks to make sure teeth and **gums** are healthy.

The Dentist Looks In

The dentist comes in to see Jordan. He checks her teeth carefully.

"Open wide," says the dentist. He looks closely to make sure Jordan's teeth and gums are healthy.

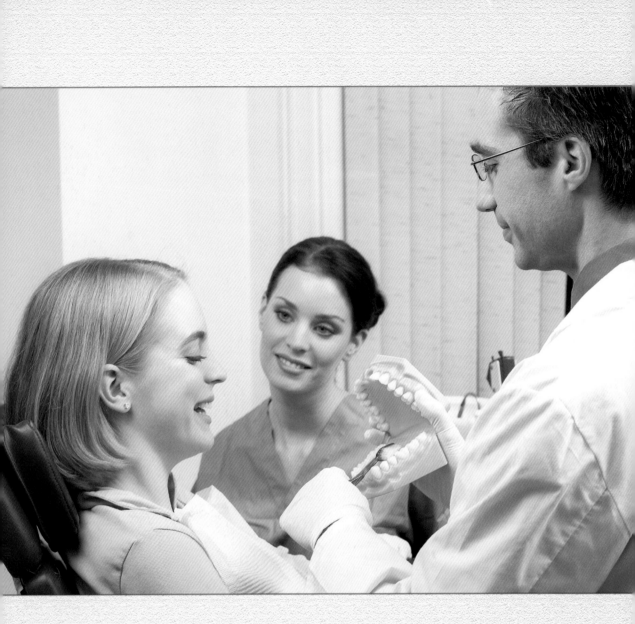

The dentist shows this patient where she may need to brush and floss more.

Brushing and Flossing

The dentist shows Jordan how to brush and floss. She practices brushing her teeth. Jordan also practices how to floss.

"Everything looks great," says the dentist.

Dentists sometimes take pictures of the inside of your mouth. These are called X rays.

The Dentist's Day

The dentist spends the whole day helping people. He tells them to brush and floss every day. Sometimes a person may have a cavity. A cavity is a bad spot on the tooth. The dentist fixes the tooth using special tools. He tells the person to stay away from sweet, sticky treats.

This dentist is talking about the day with her helper. They are getting ready for tomorrow.

Time to Go Home

At the end of the day, the waiting room is empty again. Tomorrow, more people will come. The dentist will be back, too, ready to care for his patients. At home, Jordan remembers every night to brush and floss before bedtime.

Healthy Tips

- Visit your dentist twice a year.
- Brush your teeth twice a day.
- Make sure you get every tooth.
- Floss at bedtime.
- Eat healthy foods.
- Drink milk or water.
- Show off your teeth and smile!

Learn More

Books

Bagley, Katie. *Brush Well: A Look at Dental Care*. Mankato, Minn.: Bridgestone Books, 2002.

Radabaugh, Melinda Beth. *Going to the Dentist*. Chicago, Ill.: Heinemann Library, 2004.

Swanson, Diane. *The Dentist and You*. Toronto, ON: Annick Press, 2002.

Internet Addresses

Kids Health
<http://www.kidshealth.org>
Go to the section for kids. Click on "My Body." Then click on "Teeth." Learn about the different parts of the tooth, and many other things.

Kids Stuff
<http://www.adha.org/kidstuff/index.html>
Read about your teeth and play games.

Index

Note to Teachers and Parents: The *What Does a Community Helper Do?* series supports curriculum standards for K–4 learning about community services and helpers. The Words to Know section introduces subject-specific vocabulary. Early readers may require help with these new words.

Series Literacy Consultant:
Allan A. De Fina, Ph.D.
Past President of the New Jersey Reading Association
Professor, Department of Literacy Education
New Jersey City University

Enslow Elementary, an imprint of Enslow Publishers, Inc.

Enslow Elementary® is a registered trademark
of Enslow Publishers, Inc.

Copyright © 2006 by Enslow Publishers, Inc.

Library of Congress Cataloging-in-Publication Data

Miller, Heather.
What does a dentist do? / Heather Miller.
p. cm. — (What does a community helper do?)
Includes bibliographical references and index.
ISBN 0-7660-2323-0
1. Dentists—Juvenile literature. 2. Dentistry—Juvenile literature. I. Title. II. Series.
RK63.M55 2005
617.6—dc22   2005012380

Printed in the United States of America

10 9 8 7 6 5 4 3 2 1

To Our Readers:
We have done our best to make sure all Internet Addresses in this book were active and appropriate when we went to press. However, the author and the publisher have no control over and assume no liability for the material available on those Internet sites or on other Web sites they may link to. Any comments or suggestions can be sent by e-mail to comments@enslow.com or to the address on the back cover.

Illustration Credits: brand X pictures, pp. 1, 4, 6, 8, 10, 12, 14, 18, 20; Hemera Technologies, Inc. 1997-2000, p. 11; © 2005 JupiterImages, pp. 2, 16, 22 (all).

Cover Illustration: brand X pictures (bottom); top left to right (brand X pictures, all).